The Lifestyle of Investor:

Building Wealth and Achieving Financial Freedom

DAVID WEALTH

DEDICATION

To my family, who have always been my biggest supporters and inspirations, and who have taught me the value of hard work, perseverance, and financial responsibility. This book is dedicated to you with all my love and gratitude.

May the knowledge and insights shared in this book empower you to take control of your financial future, and create a lifestyle that aligns with your values, dreams, and aspirations.

Thank you for believing in me and for being a constant source of love, encouragement, and joy. I hope this book honors your legacy and inspires you to live your best life.

With the deepest appreciation,

DAVID WEALTH

THE LIFESTYLE OF INVESTOR:

INTRODUCTION

CHAPTER 1: UNDERSTANDING INVESTING

TYPES OF INVESTMENTS
STOCKS:
BONDS
MUTUAL FUNDS
REAL ESTATE
CALCULATING RETURNS:
ROI (RETURN ON INVESTMENT)
CAGR (COMPOUND ANNUAL GROWTH RATE):
THE IMPORTANCE OF DIVERSIFICATION

CHAPTER 2: SETTING FINANCIAL GOALS

SETTING ACHIEVABLE GOALS:
CREATING A PLAN:
INVESTING IN SHORT-TERM GOALS
INVESTING FOR LONG-TERM GOALS

CHAPTER 3: CREATING A BUDGET TO SUPPORT SUCCESSFUL INVESTING

HOW TO CREATE A BUDGET:
DETERMINE YOUR INCOME:
TRACK YOUR EXPENSES:
CATEGORIZE EXPENSES
SET FINANCIAL GOALS:
ALLOCATE FUNDS:

Introduction

Investing can be an excellent way to build wealth and achieve financial freedom. However, many people don't know where to start or how to maintain a lifestyle that supports successful investing. This book aims to provide readers with a comprehensive guide on the lifestyle of an investor, from understanding the basics of investing to developing habits that can help them reach their financial goals.

Chapter 1: Understanding Investing

Investing can be a complex topic, but it's crucial to understand the basics before diving into the world of finance. In this chapter, we'll cover the fundamentals of investing, including the different types of investment options, calculating returns, and the importance of diversification.

Types of Investments: There are several types of investment options available, each with its level of risk and return. Some common types of investments include:

Stocks: Stocks represent ownership in a company and can provide capital appreciation and dividends to investors.

Bonds: Bonds are debt securities issued by governments and corporations and provide regular interest payments to investors.

Mutual funds: Mutual funds are a collection of stocks, bonds, and other assets managed by investment professionals.

Exchange-traded funds (ETFs): ETFs are like mutual funds but trade on exchanges like stocks.

Real estate: Investing in real estate can provide rental income and potential capital appreciation.

Calculating Returns:

Understanding how to calculate returns is crucial in evaluating the performance of an investment. Two common metrics used to calculate returns are:

ROI (Return on Investment):

ROI is the percentage of profit or loss on an investment relative to the initial investment.

CAGR (Compound Annual Growth Rate): CAGR is the rate of return required for an investment to grow from its initial value to its final value over a specified period.

The Importance of Diversification: Diversification is

the practice of spreading investments across different asset classes to reduce risk.

By diversifying investments, investors can reduce the impact of any single investment's performance on their overall portfolio.

A well-diversified portfolio should include investments in different asset classes, such as stocks, bonds, real estate, and commodities.

Chapter 2: Setting Financial Goals

Before embarking on an investment journey, it's crucial to set clear financial goals. In this chapter, we'll discuss the importance of setting financial goals, how to set achievable goals and creating a plan to achieve them.

Why Set Financial Goals? Setting financial goals provides direction and purpose for investing. Without clear goals, investors may make poor investment decisions or lose sight of their long-term objectives. By setting financial goals, investors can focus on what's important and create a plan to achieve them.

Setting Achievable Goals:

When setting financial goals, it's important to be realistic and specific. Vague goals such as "save more money" or "retire comfortably" are not actionable and can be challenging to achieve. Instead, goals should be specific and measurable, such as "save $10,000 for a down payment on a house in two years" or "achieve a retirement income of $60,000 per year."

Creating a Plan: Once financial

goals have been established, it's essential to create a plan to achieve them. A well-thought-out plan should include specific steps to take and a timeline for achieving each goal. Investors should also consider factors such as risk tolerance, investment horizon, and other financial obligations when creating their plans.

Investing for Short-Term Goals:
Investing for short-term goals requires a different approach than long-term goals. For example, investing for a down payment on a house in two years requires a more conservative investment approach than investing for retirement, which has a longer investment horizon. Investors should consider low-risk options such as savings accounts, money market funds, or short-term bonds for short-term goals.

Investing for Long-Term Goals:
Investing for long-term goals

such as retirement requires a different approach. Since investors have a longer investment horizon, they can take on more risk and potentially earn higher returns. Investing in stocks or stock mutual funds can be an excellent option for long-term goals, but investors should consider their risk tolerance and diversify their investments to reduce risk.

Conclusion: Setting financial goals is a critical step in achieving financial freedom and building wealth.

By setting achievable goals and creating a plan to achieve them, investors can stay focused and make informed investment decisions.

In this chapter, we discussed the importance of setting financial goals, how to set achievable goals and creating a plan to achieve them.

In the next chapter, we'll discuss creating a budget to support successful investing.

Chapter 3:

Creating a Budget to Support Successful Investing

Creating and sticking to a budget is a crucial component of successful investing. In this chapter, we'll discuss the importance of creating a budget, how to create a budget, and how to use it to support your investment goals.

Why Create a Budget? Creating a budget is the foundation of financial planning. It allows investors to track their income and expenses, identify areas where they can cut costs, and allocate funds toward achieving their financial goals. A budget provides clarity on your finances, helps to reduce financial stress, and ensures you are not overspending.

How to Create a Budget:

Creating a budget involves several steps:

Determine your income:

Calculate your total income from all sources, including salary, bonuses, and investment income.

Track your expenses: Track

your expenses for at least one month, including fixed expenses such as rent, utilities, and car payments, and variable expenses such as groceries, dining out, and entertainment.

Categorize expenses: Categorize

your expenses into necessary and

discretionary spending. Necessary spending includes expenses such as housing, utilities, and groceries, while discretionary spending includes expenses such as entertainment and travel.

Set financial goals: Set financial goals based on your priorities, such as saving for retirement or paying off debt.

Allocate funds: Allocate funds towards achieving your financial goals, while ensuring you have enough money to cover necessary expenses.

Using Your Budget to Support Investing: Once you have created a budget, you can use it to support your investment goals. Here are some tips:

Set investment goals: Use your budget to set realistic investment goals based on your income and expenses.

Prioritize investments: Allocate funds towards investments before discretionary spending.

Automate investments: Set up automatic contributions to investment accounts, such as 401(k)s or IRAs.

Revisit your budget regularly: Revisit your budget regularly and adjust as necessary to ensure you are staying on track to achieve your financial goals.

Conclusion: Creating a budget is a crucial component of successful investing. By tracking their income and expenses, setting financial goals, and allocating funds towards investments, investors can stay on track to achieve their financial objectives. In this chapter, we discussed the importance of creating a budget, how to create a budget, and how to use it to support your investment goals. In the next chapter, we'll discuss the importance of risk management in investing.

Chapter 4: The Importance of Risk Management in Investing

Investing always involves risk, and managing that risk is essential to achieving long-term success. In this chapter, we'll discuss the importance of risk management, the types of investment risks, and how to manage those risks to achieve your financial goals.

Why Is Risk Management Important?
Investing involves inherent risks, such as market volatility and economic uncertainty. Failing to manage those risks can lead to significant financial losses.

Proper risk management helps investors to mitigate those risks, reduce the impact of losses, and ensure that their investments align with their financial goals.

Types of Investment Risks:

There are several types of investment risks, including:

Market risk: The risk that changes in the stock market or other financial markets will negatively impact investment returns.

Interest rate risk: The risk that changes in interest rates will impact the value of fixed-income investments.

Credit risk: The risk that a borrower will default on a loan, impacting the value of an investment.

Inflation risk: The risk that inflation will decrease the purchasing power of investments.

Liquidity risk: The risk that an investment cannot be sold quickly or without a significant loss of value.

How to Manage Investment Risks: Here are some strategies to manage investment risks:

Diversification: Diversify investments across different asset classes, industries, and regions to reduce the impact of market fluctuations.

Asset allocation: Determine an appropriate asset allocation based on your investment goals, time horizon, and risk tolerance.

Risk tolerance assessment: Assess your risk tolerance to ensure that your investments align with your comfort level.

Stop-loss orders: Set stop-loss orders to limit losses in case of sudden market downturns.

Professional advice: Seek advice from a financial advisor or professional to ensure that your investment portfolio aligns with your financial goals and risk tolerance.

Conclusion: Investing involves inherent risks, but proper risk management can reduce the impact of those risks and ensure that investments align with your financial goals. In this chapter, we discussed the importance of risk management, the types of investment risks, and strategies to manage those risks. In the next chapter, we'll discuss the benefits of long-term investing and how to develop a long-term investment strategy.

Chapter 5: The Benefits of Long-Term Investing and Developing a Long-Term Investment Strategy

Investing is a long-term endeavor, and developing a long-term investment strategy is essential to achieving financial success. In this chapter, we'll discuss the benefits of long-term investing and how to develop a long-term investment strategy.

The Benefits of Long-Term Investing

: Long-term investing offers several benefits, including:

Compounding: Compounding allows investors to earn returns on their initial investment and any subsequent earnings, resulting in exponential growth over time.

Time in the market: By staying invested for the long term, investors can ride out short-term market fluctuations and benefit from overall market growth.

Lower transaction costs: Frequent trading and portfolio turnover can lead to higher transaction costs, which can eat into investment returns. Long-term investing reduces the need for frequent trading and lowers transaction costs.

Developing a Long-Term Investment Strategy: Here are some steps to developing a long-term investment strategy:

Determine your investment goals: Identify your financial goals, such as retirement or saving for a down payment on a home.

Assess your risk tolerance: Assess your risk tolerance to ensure that your investment strategy aligns with your comfort level.

Determine your investment time horizon: Consider your investment time horizon, which is the length of time you plan to hold your investments.

Choose appropriate investments: Choose investments that align with your investment goals, risk tolerance, and investment time horizon.

Stick to your investment plan: Avoid making frequent changes to your investment plan and remain disciplined in your approach.

Rebalance your portfolio: Rebalance your portfolio periodically to ensure that it aligns with your investment goals and risk tolerance.

Conclusion: Long-term investing offers several benefits, including compounding, time in the market, and lower transaction costs. Developing a long-term investment strategy involves determining your investment goals, assessing your risk tolerance, choosing appropriate investments, and sticking to your investment plan. In the next chapter, we'll discuss the importance of staying informed about market trends and economic indicators.

Chapter 6: Staying Informed About Market Trends and Economic Indicators

Investing requires a deep understanding of market trends and economic indicators. In this chapter, we'll discuss the importance of staying informed about market trends and economic indicators, the key indicators to watch, and how to use this information to inform your investment decisions.

Why Is Staying Informed About Market Trends and

Economic Indicators

Important? Staying informed about market trends and economic indicators is essential to making informed investment decisions. Economic indicators provide insights into the overall health of the economy, which can impact the performance of individual companies and sectors. Market trends can also provide insights into the performance of individual stocks and the overall market.

Key Economic Indicators to

Watch: Here are some key economic indicators to watch:

Gross Domestic Product (GDP): GDP measures the total value of goods and services produced in a country and is a key indicator of economic health.

Unemployment rate: The unemployment rate measures the percentage of people who are actively seeking employment but cannot find a job.

Inflation rate: The inflation rate measures the rate of increase in the prices of goods and services over time.

Consumer confidence: Consumer confidence measures the overall optimism of consumers regarding their finances and the economy.

Interest rates: Interest rates can impact the performance of fixed-income investments, such as bonds.

Corporate earnings: The earnings of individual companies provide insights into their financial health and performance.

How to Use Market Trends and Economic Indicators to Inform Investment

Decisions: Here are some tips on how to use market trends and economic indicators to inform investment decisions:

Consider the impact on individual stocks: Economic indicators can impact the performance of individual stocks and sectors, so consider how changes in the economy may impact the companies you're invested in.

Look for long-term trends: Short-term fluctuations can be misleading, so look for long-term trends to inform your investment decisions.

Consider the current economic environment: Economic indicators should be viewed in the context of the current economic environment. For example, high inflation may be expected during a period of economic growth, but it may be cause for concern during a period of economic stagnation.

Seek professional advice: Consider seeking advice from a financial advisor or professional to ensure that you're interpreting market trends and economic indicators correctly.

Conclusion: Staying informed about market trends and economic indicators is essential to making informed investment decisions. Key economic indicators to watch include GDP, unemployment rate, inflation rate, consumer confidence, interest rates, and corporate earnings. Use this information to inform your investment decisions, but remember to consider the long-term trends and seek professional advice.

Chapter 7:
Diversification and Asset Allocation

Diversification and asset allocation are critical components of a successful investment strategy. In this chapter, we'll discuss the importance of diversification and asset allocation, the different types of investments, and how to develop a diversified portfolio.

The Importance of Diversification and Asset Allocation: Diversification and asset allocation are important for two main reasons:

Risk management:

Diversification helps to manage risk by spreading your investments across different types of assets, reducing the impact of any one investment on your overall portfolio.

Performance optimization:

Asset allocation involves dividing your investments among different asset classes to optimize your portfolio's overall performance.

Types of Investments: There are three main types of investments:

Equities: Equities, also known as stocks, represent ownership in a company and offer the potential for growth and income.

Fixed-income: Fixed-income investments, such as bonds, offer a fixed rate of return and are generally less volatile than equities.

Cash and cash equivalents: Cash and cash equivalents, such as money market funds, provide stability and liquidity but generally offer lower returns.

Developing a Diversified Portfolio: Here are some tips for developing a diversified portfolio:

Consider your investment goals: Identify your investment goals and risk tolerance to determine the appropriate asset allocation for your portfolio.

Allocate your investments: Divide your investments among different asset classes, such as equities, fixed income, and cash and cash equivalents, based on your risk tolerance and investment goals.

Diversify within asset classes: Diversify within each asset class by investing in different companies, industries, and geographies.

Monitor and rebalance your portfolio: Monitor your portfolio regularly and rebalance as needed to maintain your desired asset allocation.

Consider professional advice: Consider seeking advice from a financial advisor or professional to ensure that your portfolio is properly diversified and aligned with your investment goals.

Conclusion: Diversification and asset allocation are essential components of a successful investment strategy. By investing in different types of assets and diversifying within each asset class, investors can manage risk and optimize portfolio performance. Consider your investment goals and risk tolerance, allocate your investments among different asset classes, diversify within asset classes, and monitor and rebalance your portfolio regularly.

Chapter 8: Tax Planning for Investors

Tax planning is an important consideration for investors, as taxes can have a significant impact on investment returns. In this chapter, we'll discuss the importance of tax planning, strategies for minimizing taxes, and how to optimize your investments for tax efficiency.

The Importance of Tax Planning

: Taxes can significantly impact investment returns, so it's important to consider tax implications when making investment decisions. Effective tax planning can help investors minimize tax liabilities and maximize after-tax returns.

Strategies for Minimizing Taxes:

Here are some strategies for minimizing taxes:

Invest in tax-advantaged accounts: Tax-advantaged accounts, such as 401(k)s, IRAs, and HSAs, offer tax benefits that can reduce your tax liabilities and increase your after-tax returns.

Harvest losses: Tax-loss harvesting involves selling investments that have lost value to offset gains from other investments and reduce your tax liabilities.

Consider tax-efficient investments: Some investments, such as index funds and municipal bonds, are more tax-efficient than others and can help reduce your tax liabilities.

Time investment sales: Holding investments for more than one year can qualify for long-term capital gains tax rates, which are generally lower than short-term capital gains tax rates.

Optimizing Investments for Tax Efficiency: Here are some tips for optimizing your investments for tax efficiency:

Consider asset location: Placing tax-inefficient investments, such as bonds, in tax-advantaged accounts and tax-efficient investments, such as equities, in taxable accounts, can help optimize your investments for tax efficiency.

Rebalance tax-efficiently: When rebalancing your portfolio, consider the tax implications of selling investments and aim to minimize tax liabilities.

Use tax-efficient investment vehicles: Exchange-traded funds (ETFs) and mutual funds that are specifically designed to be tax-efficient can help optimize your investments for tax efficiency.

Consult with a tax professional: Tax laws and regulations can be complex, so consider consulting with a tax professional to ensure that you're optimizing your investments for tax efficiency.

Conclusion: Effective tax planning is an important consideration for investors. By investing in tax-advantaged accounts, harvesting losses, considering tax-efficient investments, and optimizing investments for tax efficiency, investors can minimize tax liabilities and maximize after-tax returns. Consider asset location, rebalancing tax-efficiently, using tax-efficient investment vehicles, and consulting with a tax professional to ensure that you're optimizing your investments for tax efficiency.

Chapter 9:
Investing for Retirement

Investing for retirement is a critical component of long-term financial planning. In this chapter, we'll discuss the importance of investing for retirement, different types of retirement accounts, and strategies for building a retirement portfolio.

The Importance of Investing for Retirement: Investing for retirement is important for several reasons:

Long-term financial security: Investing for retirement ensures that you have enough money to support yourself during retirement.

Inflation protection: Investing for retirement can help protect against inflation by earning a return on your investments that outpaces inflation.

Tax advantages: Retirement accounts offer tax advantages that can reduce your tax liabilities and increase your after-tax returns.

Types of Retirement Accounts: Here are some common types of retirement accounts:

401(k) and 403(b) plan: Employer-sponsored retirement plans that allow employees to contribute a portion of their pre-tax income to a retirement account.

Traditional IRA: A tax-deferred retirement account that allows individuals to contribute pre-tax dollars and defer taxes until retirement.

Roth IRA: A retirement account that allows individuals to contribute after-tax dollars and withdraw earnings tax-free in retirement.

Pension plans: Employer-sponsored retirement plans that provide a defined benefit to retirees based on their years of service and salary.

Strategies for Building a Retirement Portfolio: Here are some strategies for building a retirement portfolio:

Start early: The earlier you start investing for retirement, the more time your investments must grow.

Diversify your portfolio: Diversification helps to manage risk by spreading your investments across different types of assets.

Consider your risk tolerance: Your risk tolerance should guide your investment decisions, balancing the need for growth with the need for stability.

Review and rebalance regularly: Review your retirement portfolio regularly and rebalance as needed to maintain your desired asset allocation.

Consider professional advice: Consider seeking advice from a financial advisor or professional to ensure that your retirement portfolio is aligned with your goals and risk tolerance.

Conclusion: Investing for retirement is a critical component of long-term financial planning. Retirement accounts offer tax advantages and protect against inflation, and strategies such as starting early, diversifying your portfolio, and reviewing and rebalancing regularly can help build a successful retirement portfolio. Consider your risk tolerance, seek professional advice, and start investing for retirement as early as possible to maximize your long-term financial security.

Chapter 10: The Importance of a Long-Term Investment Mindset

Investing with a long-term mindset is essential for achieving financial goals and building wealth over time. In this chapter, we'll discuss the importance of a long-term investment mindset and strategies for developing and maintaining it.

The Importance of a Long-Term Investment Mindset:

Here are some reasons why a long-term investment mindset is important:

Time horizon: Long-term investing allows for the power of compounding, which can lead to significant wealth accumulation over time.

Emotions: Short-term market volatility can be emotionally challenging, and a long-term mindset can help investors stay focused on their goals and avoid impulsive decisions.

Risk management: A long-term mindset can help investors manage risk by focusing on the long-term fundamentals of an investment rather than short-term market fluctuations.

Strategies for Developing and Maintaining a Long-Term Investment Mindset:

Here are some strategies for developing

and maintaining a long-term investment mindset:

Define your goals: Clearly define your investment goals and create a plan to achieve them.

Stay disciplined: Stick to your investment plan and resist the urge to make impulsive decisions based on short-term market fluctuations.

Diversify your portfolio: Diversification can help manage risk and maintain a long-term focus.

Focus on fundamentals: Focus on the long-term fundamentals of an investment rather than short-term market fluctuations.

Stay informed: Stay informed about the economy, market trends, and developments in your investments, but avoid becoming overly reactive to short-term news.

epilogue: A long-term investment mindset is essential for achieving financial goals and building wealth over time. It allows for the power of compounding, helps manage risk, and helps investors avoid emotional decisions based on short-term market fluctuations. Define your goals, stay disciplined, diversify your portfolio, focus on fundamentals, and stay informed to develop and maintain a long-term investment mindset. By doing so, you can achieve your financial goals and build a successful investment portfolio.

Bibliography

David, T. (2016). The Automatic Millionaire: A Powerful One-Step Plan to Live and Finish Rich. New York: Crown Business.

Kiyosaki, R. (2017). Rich Dad Poor Dad: What the Rich Teach Their Kids About Money That the Poor and Middle Class Do Not! New York: Plata Publishing.

Lynch, P., & Rothchild, J. (2011). One up on Wall Street: How to Use What You Already Know to Make Money in the Market. New York: Simon & Schuster.

Reference page

David, T. (2016). The Automatic Millionaire: A Powerful One-Step Plan to Live and Finish Rich. New York: Crown Business.

Kiyosaki, R. (2017). Rich Dad Poor Dad: What the Rich Teach Their Kids About Money That the Poor and Middle Class Do Not! New York: Plata Publishing.

Lynch, P., & Rothchild, J. (2011). One up on Wall Street: How to Use What You Already Know to Make Money in the Market. New York: Simon & Schuster.

ABOUT THE AUTHOR

David is an accomplished author, speaker, and entrepreneur who is passionate about helping people live their best life. With over 24 years of experience in Finance, David has a wealth of knowledge and expertise that he shares with his/her readers through his books.

David's writing style is engaging, inspiring, and practical, and he has a talent for turning complex concepts into simple, easy-to-understand terms.

In addition to his writing, David is a sought-after speaker and coach, having delivered inspiring keynotes and workshops to audiences around the world. He has a passion for helping people achieve their full potential, and his/her message of empowerment and personal growth has resonated with thousands of people.

When he is not writing or speaking, David enjoys reading and spending time with his family and friends. He believes in living life to the fullest and making every moment count.

Through his work, David continues to inspire and motivate people to pursue their dreams, overcome their fears, and create a life that they love

INDEX